NIC BISHOP
SNAKES

Written and photographed by
Nic Bishop
Scholastic Inc.

Snakes are scary and strange.

They have long, thin bodies and wriggle on their bellies.

They can climb to the treetops
without the help of arms or legs.

The largest snakes are anacondas and pythons.

Some are big enough to swallow a whole pig.

Blind snakes are as tiny as worms.

They slither underground and eat insects.

Snakes have super senses.

They can taste scent trails with their forked tongues and follow them to find *prey*.

They can feel vibrations through their bodies to know when an animal moves nearby.

Some snakes can even pinpoint prey in total darkness.

The emerald tree boa has heat-sensing organs to "see" the warm body of an opossum at night.

But the scariest part is how snakes kill their prey.

Many lie in wait to *ambush*.

Some wrap their victim in powerful coils and squeeze until even its blood stops moving.

Other snakes have deadly *venom*,
which they inject with fangs.

Then the snake swallows its prey whole. The jawbones open wide and the snake's mouth stretches over its food.

This snake is swallowing an egg four times bigger than its head.

A large meal will last a snake for weeks, or even months.

The snake will keep out of sight while it digests its food. It has to watch out for danger.

Some mammals, birds, and even other snakes will eat snakes.

But a snake can defend itself.

The hognose snake pretends to be
dead and poops bad-tasting goo.

Venomous snakes will bite, fast. The king cobra has enough venom to kill an elephant.

Some snakes pretend to be more dangerous than they really are.

Brightly colored king snakes often look like deadly venomous coral snakes.

The best defense is not to be seen.

The Gaboon viper looks just like leaves.

Snakes will hide their eggs, too.

The mother snake often lays her eggs under logs, in a tree hole, or even in an old burrow.

The young will hatch several weeks later, ready for their first meal.

A Closer Look with Nic Bishop

Snakes are shy, nervous, and fast. And they do not want to stay in one place while their picture is being taken. I really wanted to show how beautiful snakes are. So I used lighting that would capture the wonderful colors of their scaly skins. I also wanted to photograph the snakes face-to-face to bring readers into their world.

Many of the snakes in this book were photographed in captivity, which gave me time to set up my equipment properly. Photographing venomous snakes can be dangerous, so I placed a sheet of glass between myself and the Mojave rattlesnake. For other venomous snakes, I used a lens that allowed me to stay out of range. And I was always helped by a snake expert. Fortunately, most of the snakes I photographed were quite well behaved.

Glossary

ambush: to lie in wait and attack by surprise

prey: an animal that is hunted by another animal for food

venom: a poison that passes into a victim's body through a bite or sting

Photo Index

parrot snake,
page 1

Mandarin rat snake,
pages 2–3

green tree python,
pages 4–5

yellow anaconda,
page 6

blind snake,
page 7

Mojave rattlesnake,
pages 8–9

emerald tree boa,
pages 10–11, 32

Asian sand viper,
page 12

carpet python,
page 13

eyelash viper,
pages 14–15

African egg-eating snake,
page 17

rainbow boa,
pages 18–19

hognose snake,
page 20

king cobra,
page 21

king snake,
pages 22–23

Gaboon viper,
pages 24–25

Honduran milk snake,
pages 26–27

African horned bush viper,
page 29